I0813155

An Imprint of Pop!
popbooksonline.com

THE RED era

Track List

1. State of Grace
2. Red
3. Treacherous
4. I Knew You Were Trouble
5. All Too Well
6. 22
7. I Almost Do
8. We Are Never Ever Getting Back Together
9. Stay Stay Stay
10. The Last Time (ft. Gary Lightbody)
11. Holy Ground
12. Sad Beautiful Tragic
13. The Lucky One
14. Everything Has Changed (ft. Ed Sheeran)
15. Starlight
16. Begin Again

by Elizabeth Andrews

WELCOME TO DiscoverRoo!

This book is filled with videos, puzzles, games, and more! Scan the QR codes* while you read, or visit the website below to make this book pop.

popbooksonline.com/Red

abdobooks.com

Published by Pop!, a division of ABDO, PO Box 398166, Minneapolis, Minnesota 55439.

Printed in the United States of America, North Mankato, Minnesota.

082025
012026

Cover Photo: Alexandra Tarasova (BigArtLab); ShutterstockImages

Interior Photos: Getty Images; PaoloV/Flickr; Shutterstock Images; Storms Media Group/Alamy Stock Photo; ZUMA Press, Inc./Alamy Stock Photo

Editor: Grace Hansen and Anna Schwartz

Series Designer: Laura Graphenteen

Library of Congress Control Number: 2025941225

Publisher's Cataloging-in-Publication Data

Names: Andrews, Elizabeth, author.

Title: The Red era / by Elizabeth Andrews

Description: Minneapolis, Minnesota : Pop!, 2026 | Series: The eras of Taylor Swift | Includes online resources and index

Identifiers: ISBN 9781098248734 (lib. bdg.) | ISBN 9781098249250 (ebook)

Subjects: LCSH: Swift, Taylor, 1989- --Juvenile literature. | Popular music--Juvenile literature. | Popular (Songs, etc.)--Juvenile literature. | Albums--Juvenile literature. | Concerts--Juvenile literature. | Mass media and music--Juvenile literature.

Classification: DDC 782.42164098--dc23

*Scanning QR codes requires a web-enabled smart device with a QR code reader app and a camera.

TABLE OF CONTENTS

CHAPTER 1

NEVER EVER GOING BACK

Taylor Swift was finishing the Speak Now World Tour in 2012. She had been a global superstar for five years. She wasn't slowing down! On August 13, 2012, Taylor released a new **single** during a livestream with fans. It was called "We Are Never Ever Getting Back Together" ("WANEGBT").

WATCH A VIDEO HERE!

Meet Taylor

Birthday: December 13, 1989
Star Sign: Sagittarius
Place of Birth: West Reading, PA
Favorite Number: 13
Favorite Color: Purple
Favorite Meal: Chicken tenders and a chocolate shake

Meredith Grey

13

Benjamin Button

XOXO

Olivia Benson

Taylor Swift

Taylor Swift performed "WANEGBT" live on television for the first time during the MTV Video Music Awards.

Immediately, fans heard a difference in Taylor's sound. "WANEGBT" had more pop **influence** than anything Taylor had released before. She worked with two new **producers** on the single. They were Shellback and Max Martin. They make dance-pop tunes. Things were changing for the country music sweetheart.

The lyrics in "WANEGBT" make it clear that Taylor and her partner broke up and got back together often. Taylor said her inspiration for the song came when one of her ex's friends showed up at her recording **studio** and told her they heard the couple would be getting back together soon. "WANEGBT" is most likely about Taylor's ex Jake Gyllenhaal.

Hidden Message

The hidden message in "WANEGBT" was "When I stopped caring what you thought." Taylor was much younger than Jake. She sings about looking for his approval.

Taylor's circus ringleader outfit may have been inspired by how crazy her life felt at the time.

The music video for "WANEGBT" was different from anything she had done before too. It is a one-shot video. This means the video was filmed in one take by one camera. There are a lot of silly things that happen in the video to take attention away from Taylor while she changes costumes.

Taylor changed her hair during the Red Era. She started wearing it straight most of the time.

CHAPTER 2

RED

Taylor wrote and recorded 25 songs within a year of *Speak Now*'s release. Her **label** thought this was plenty of material to complete her fourth **studio** album. But Taylor wasn't satisfied. She wanted to try something new!

EXPLORE LINKS HERE!

RED
TAYLOR SWIFT

Red sold 1.2 million copies in its first week of sales.

Red was released on October 22, 2012, through Big Machine Records. Unlike her last two albums, not all the songs on *Red* were **produced** with Nathan Chapman. He worked on 8 of the final 16 tracks. Taylor chose to work with new producers. They helped Taylor add dance and pop music to the album.

Taylor is listed as a producer on Red.

Dubstep has a heavier sound than other electronic music.

Even before *Red* was released, Swifties were nervous about what the album would be like. They knew she was mixing in dubstep, electronic, and dance pop with her traditional **genres** of country and rock. *Red* was well received. People applauded her continuous growth in songcraft. Her fans were divided on whether they liked the new genre **influences**.

Ed Sheeran sings on Red. He joined Taylor for the album's tour.

Red is a breakup album with small bits of hope at the end. Taylor showed the complicated and difficult feelings that come when love fades away. This was her first album that shifted from the dreamy kind of love and instead faced the hard truths of relationships.

Eventually, listeners realized how wonderful the album was. It spent seven weeks at number 1 on the Billboard Top 100. The album won at the American Music Awards, Billboard Awards, and Academy of Country Music Awards. *Red* was also nominated for Album of the Year at the 2014 **Grammy Awards**.

Taylor's favorite number is 13. She often displays it during performances.

CHAPTER 3

BEHIND THE LYRICS

Some of the more emotional songs on *Red* are "Treacherous," "I Almost Do," and "State of Grace." These songs are likely about Taylor's relationship and break-ups with Jake Gyllenhaal. The couple was on-again, off-again according to "WANEGBT."

COMPLETE AN ACTIVITY HERE!

All the emotions from that pattern gave Taylor song material for the album.

Taylor went to London to work on music for Red.

Red *Era* fashion featured trends from the 1950s and 1960s.

After "WANEGBT" came out as the first **single**, Taylor released a new song from *Red* every Tuesday until the entire album dropped. “Begin Again” was the second single. Unlike the breakup bop before it, “Begin Again” is a sweet country tune at the end of the album. It is widely believed to be about Connor Kennedy and the hope she felt after meeting him.

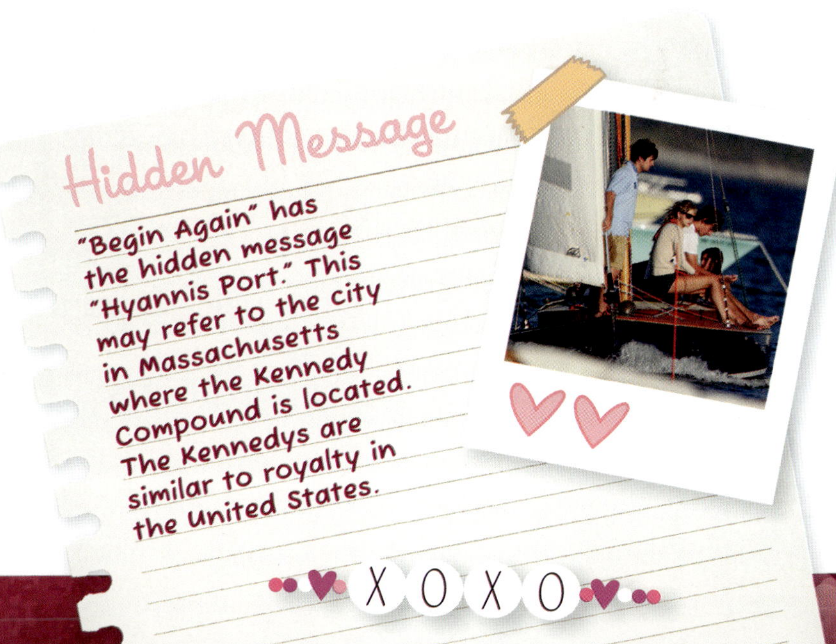

Harry Styles was a member of the band One Direction.

"I Knew You Were Trouble" ("IKYWT") is rumored to be about Harry Styles. Its hidden message is "When you saw me dancing." Swifties think it hints at when Harry saw Taylor and her friend Selena Gomez dancing to his band at the 2012 Kids Choice Awards. "IKYWT" was very different from Taylor's old music. It spent seven weeks at the top of pop charts.

"22" was another single off *Red*. It fit in with the bubblegum-pop music of the time. When the album came out, Taylor said that 22 was her favorite year of life. She felt old enough to start planning for her future but young enough to feel carefree. This song's hidden message is "Ashley Dianna Claire Selena." Those are the names of some of her best friends at the time.

On the Eras Tour, Taylor wore a sparkly version of the T-shirt she wore in the "22" music video.

CHAPTER 4

RED RECLAIMED

Taylor Swift and her band took *Red* on tour starting March 13, 2013, in Omaha, Nebraska. It was another world tour, with 86 shows at **stadiums** and arenas. She brought along country and pop **openers** that included Ed Sheeran, The

LEARN MORE HERE!

Vamps, and Florida Georgia Line. In its review of the tour, the magazine *Rolling Stone* said no other pop act could come close to entertaining the way Taylor does.

The Red Tour was attended by 1.7 million people.

Miles Teller was the male lead in the "I Bet You Think About Me" video. Taylor is close with him and his wife.

Red (Taylor's Version) was released on November 12, 2021. It was her second rerecorded album. Taylor didn't offer fans many Easter eggs before announcing the album on June 18, 2021. But some

Easter eggs are secret messages and clues in Taylor's work.

fans noticed she used four red hearts in a social media post. She also used lyrics from *Red* when posting about songs from her ninth album, *evermore.*

Songs "From the Vault" are tracks that Taylor recorded for the original album but didn't release. They are included on Taylor's Versions.

There were nine tracks "From the Vault" on *Red (Taylor's Version)*. The first **single** was "I Bet You Think About Me." The music video was released the night before the rerecording dropped. It features country music star Chris Stapleton. Fans believe this song is about Jake Gyllenhaal.

After the cover for *Red (Taylor's Version)* was released, fans saw that Taylor was wearing the same outfit that she had on in the art for her song "Long Story Short."

WHAT THE FANS WANT

"All Too Well" sits as track five on *Red*. The fifth songs on Taylor's albums are the saddest. Taylor wrote "All Too Well" during concert rehearsal. She played her guitar and her band joined her. The lyrics flowed out. "All Too Well" was the longest song on *Red*. She doubled its playing time on *Taylor's Version*. The song is about everything that Taylor remembers all too well from her past relationship.

"All Too Well (10 Minute Version) (Taylor's Version)" was the biggest hit off the rerecorded album. The song was a fan favorite from *Red*. When the 10-minute song came out, it gave Swifties even more of what they loved—her heartfelt and emotional lyrics. Taylor wrote and directed the music video for the song. It won the 2022 **Grammy** for Best Music Video.

Dylan O'Brien and Sadie Sink starred in the "All Too Well (10 Minute Version) (Taylor's Version)" music video.

MAKING CONNECTIONS

TEXT-TO-SELF

What is your favorite song from the *Red* Era? Why is it your favorite?

TEXT-TO-TEXT

Have you read books about any other music artists? How are they similar to or different from Taylor Swift?

TEXT-TO-WORLD

As a reader, why do you think so many people around the world connect with Taylor Swift and her music? Write a few sentences to explain your answer.

GLOSSARY

genre — a type of music. Country, rock, and jazz are examples of music genres.

Grammy Awards — an event that recognizes and awards remarkable works in music throughout the year. The award given is called a Grammy.

influence — the power of a thing that causes an effect on another.

label — a company that helps make and release music recordings.

opener — a performer who comes on stage before the main act.

produce — to organize the creation of music recordings. A person who produces is a producer.

single — a song that is released as a stand-alone from the album.

stadium — a place used for events, that has rows of seats rising up around an open field.

studio — a place where recordings are made.

INDEX

DiscoverRoo!
ONLINE RESOURCES

This book is filled with videos, puzzles, games, and more! Scan the QR codes* while you read, or visit the website below to make this book pop.

popbooksonline.com/Red

*Scanning QR codes requires a web-enabled smart device with a QR code reader app and a camera.